A Crown of Violets

A Crown of Violets

Renée Vivien

Translated by

Samantha Pious

Headmistress Press

ISBN-13: 978-0692536919
ISBN-10: 0692536914

Cover art by Louise Abbéma, *Une élégante, place de la Concorde*
(c. 1894), Licensed by Carnavalet Museum, Paris.
Cover & book design by Mary Meriam.

P U B L I S H E R

Headmistress Press
60 Shipview Lane
Sequim, WA 98382
Telephone: 917-428-8312
Email: headmistresspress@gmail.com
Website: headmistresspress.blogspot.com

For Sara Weil

CONTENTS

PREFACE

American readers, particularly college students, have heard of Renée Vivien (1877-1909) both as the tragic, suicidal lesbian lover of the witty, wealthy salon hostess Natalie Clifford Barney, and as an eccentric Englishwoman who insisted on writing verses in French. These legends could not be more wrong. Vivien is the author of an extraordinary body of short stories, epigrams, plays, satires, a *roman à clef,* translations, and poetry (in both prose and verse) concerning her feelings of alienation and exile, her sexual and existential anxieties, and her longing for erotic, spiritual, and artistic transcendence.

Vivien was one of the first women poets of modern European literary history to portray lesbianism sympathetically for a female audience. Her work was a deliberate, courageous transgression against the tacit prohibition against women writing about love between women. Vivien did nothing to disguise this transgression; on the contrary, she affirmed it. Her vision criticized heterosexuality, rejected marriage, celebrated infertility and virginity, and rebelled against the divine laws of a patriarchal, oppressive God.

Through her writing, Vivien successfully traced a genealogy of lesbian literature and legend, a subversive history of powerful, transgressive women. Her poetry evokes and intertwines the diverse figures of Aphrodite and Venus, Sappho and her lover Atthis, the enchantress Viviane of Arthurian legend, Shakespeare's Ophelia and other drowned women, the tragic Anne Boleyn, Dante's Beatrice, the

Virgin Mary, and the biblical Lilith and Vashti. In effect, she was performing feminist archival research sixty years before the advent of modern feminist scholarship.

Today, Vivien's work could pose important challenges to queer and feminist theory. While today's scholars devote themselves to dismantling binary oppositions, especially the "gender binary" between masculine and feminine, Vivien valorizes such dichotomies while manipulating them for her own subversive ends. Many of her poems offer fascinating perspectives on the ideas of "queer time" and "queer space," and others deeply resonate with the theories of scholars such as Judith Butler, Lee Edelman, and Heather Love. Her poetic adaptations of Sappho and other Ancient Greek women poets perform striking feats of literary-historical research several decades *before* the heyday of feminist recovery projects in the 1970s.

Vivien offers a terrible temptation for any woman translator: to see herself not only as a literary successor but also as a *lover,* in the most literal sense of the word, of Renée Vivien. It was a temptation I did not resist. Sometimes, when verses and stanzas came particularly easily, I would imagine that it was Vivien herself who was composing through my hands — that I was hearing her voice in my mind — as though I were some sort of Spiritualist medium. The vocabulary errors in my early drafts, which I have since corrected, would suggest a deathly silence on Vivien's part. (But then, she always was reserved.)

Sandia Belgrade, who translated Vivien's 1906 volume *À l'Heure des Mains jointes* as *At the Sweet Hour of Hand in Hand* (The Naiad Press, 1979), portrays her relationship

2

with Vivien in these terms:

> I have held Renée Vivien in my arms at times, and in
> some strange way she has been a part of my own
> expiation. Some intermingling of time and space, an
> erotic continuum that joins our lives to each other —
> erotic. [...] To understand Vivien and our relationship to
> the whole feminine lineage, we must see eroticism not
> just in its limited sexual sense, but in a more expansive
> way that includes the full range of love. (xii)

There is an urge to rescue Vivien, to comfort her as though
she truly were a lost child. Although my own translations are
substantially different from Belgrade's, I have also
experienced this sensual, even physical feeling of — shall
we call it possessiveness? — the feeling that Vivien was *my*
lover, *my* sister, *my* child. It was only with reluctance that I
could bring myself to glance through Belgrade's and other
translations. Once I did so, it became patently clear that
Vivien did not speak to me alone.

Although it is still possible to purchase copies of the
English translations by Belgrade, Karla Jay, and others,
these volumes are growing more and more difficult to find.
In addition, English-language anthologies of
lesbian/women's literature offer a scant selection of Vivien's
poetry. My translations are an effort at increasing her
accessibility, so that you, too, may hear her siren song.

Samantha Pious
August, 2015

VICTORY

Donne-moi tes baisers amers comme des larmes

Give me kisses bitter as your tears tonight,
When birds pause in their flight to wait.
Our long loveless unions have the charms
Of plunder, and the feral lure of rape.

Your eyes reflect the splendor of the storm ...
Breathe out your scorn until you swoon away,
My very dear! — Unclose your lips in wrath:
I'll slowly drink their poison and their rage.

Roused as a pirate before his precious spoils,
Tonight when all your gaze's glow has fled,
The conqueror's soul, savage and radiant,
Sings in my triumph as I leave your bed!

AMAZON

L'Amazone sourit au dessus des ruines

The Amazon smiles above the ruins, while
The sun, weary of warfare, sinks to rest.
Of voluptuous murder she has had her fill:
She exults, strange woman, amorous of death.

She loves only lovers who offer her their mad
Wild agony and their fierce, proud fall,
And, scorning honeyed, watery caresses,
She doesn't care for lukewarm lips at all.

Her desire, on some pallid mouth descending,
Rends one last kiss from lips gone still, above
The raspy, ghastly gasp — the final spasm —
More fearful and more fair than that of love.

PROPHECY

Tes cheveux aux blonds verts s'imprègnent d'émeraude

Your green-blond hair basks in an emerald glow
Beneath the bright and verdant sky.
The scent of poppies lingers in the air
And prowls, like a slowly dying sigh.
My eyes fixed on your slender smile,
I marvel at its cleverness and cruelty,
But, pierced with visions of the years to come,
As though a prophet, I lament your beauty!

Since such is the stupid, sorrowful law,
Even you, my lily, shall wither up at last!
And in the wrinkled furrow's public shame,
Your brow shall bear but one sign only: *Past!*
The rhythm of the sea shall leave your steps;
Your limbs and body, wasted through and through,
Shall no more shiver in desire's depths,
And Love itself no longer speak to you.

No longer, in the sorrow of your generous heart,
Shall your breast quiver like a wing in flight,
And you shall flee the cruel, exquisite hour
When lovers' brows pale in the dying light.
Your sleep will always fear the setting sun,
The last light of the last flame, and your soul,
A sad and loving virgin, shall extinguish
In eyes as dark as tombstones and more cold.

Gray Eyes

Le charme de tes yeux sans couleur ni lumière

The magic of your colorless and lightless eyes
Captures me; it's growing sad and late,
And, lost beneath the fold of your pale lids,
Betwixt your shadowed lashes lies your gaze.

And I interrogate your pupils' stagnant pools.
They have the void of winter, dusk, and graves:
I see eternal Limbos drifting there,
The terrible, dull endlessness of ocean waves.

Nothing lives within you, not one tender dream.
Your dark, soulless eyes extinguish all you see,
As though a silent home, an ashy fireside ...
And time grows tedious as a rosary.

And in your dismal sight's despondency,
I feel a cold contempt for the living and the strong ...
Within your eyes I've found the stillness and the death
One breathes from sleeping near the dead too long.

DESIRE

Elle est lasse, après tant d'épuisantes luxures.

She's weary, worn out from so much lust.
The perfume emanating from her agonized
Limbs recalls their bruises. Debauchery
Has hollowed out her shadowy blue eyes.

And the fever of those longed-for nights
Makes her pale gold tresses still more pale.
Her body has a restive languidness.
But now the Lover with the cruel long nails

Comes suddenly to seize, to clasp, to grasp her,
With such savage and such gentle fire
That the fair broken body opens as it pleads,
In a wail of love, of dread, and of desire.

And the sob that rises in a monotone,
Finally gone mad on such voluptuousness,
Howls as one howls in moments of agony
And cannot hope to move the vast impassiveness.

Then, the sharp strangling of the plaintive voice,
The fearful silence, bringing dread that lingers,
And on the neck, as though on some dead stem,
The pallid, green-tinged markings of her fingers.

THE DROWNED WOMEN

Voici l'heure de brume où flottent les noyées

Now is the hour when the drowned arise,
Like water lilies whose white bloom has fled.
Their gowns are full and wide as unfurled sails
That will not see their harbor's home again.

Strange flowers of the sea, in strange array,
Their limbs are long and snaking, and they flow
With the slow, lazy rhythm of the tides;
The eddies set their dark, dead eyes aglow.

Like seaweed made of amber or of gold,
Their hair spreads into lacework fluidly;
Their souls are like the conches that enclose
The sea's uncertain, moving harmony.

They love the nights of agony and storm
Whose breath devours ships: they are the final sight
Of dying men, the moment of the wreck,
Before the moon's last gleam has taken flight.

They spread their feverish and loving hands,
They spread their hands in token of a plea;
Their marriage bed, within the happy depths,
Uncloses, fragrant with the salty sea.

They love the nights in which there still persists
The daylight's languor and its ecstasy,
The burning summer nights of stars and flame,
When dreams flee toward stark sensuality,

When Sappho of Lesbos, their pale sovereign,
Sings Aphrodite who corrupts the kiss
And mingles with desire all the shock of hate,
Aphrodite rising from the unslaked abyss,

Powerful Aphrodite, with her rage divine,
Whose solemn accents she has learned to sing,
The ardent, boundless love of female lips,
Of naked breasts and virgins trembling ...

FURS

Je hume en frémissant la tiédeur animale

I shiver, breathing in the warmth of furs
the blue of silver, or the blue of pearls;
I taste their scent, still stronger than the tastes
Of voices blaspheming in rut or blood,
And with an equal lust, I venerate
The Woman whom I fear, the Wildness that I love.

My sensual hands glide through the gentle Furs,
Shivering as the sharp suspicion stirs
Of frightened beasts that flee the hunting calls.
My northern dream seeks out the frigid skies
Whose gray enchants me and whose cold enthralls
And woods where snowdrifts sleep like long goodbyes.

For I am one of those whom cold makes wild.
I laughed at hoarfrost's radiance as a child.
I triumph in the wind, I glory in the storms,
I love to contemplate the tempests face to face.
I am a daughter of the Ice and of the North, —
I've often dreamed of sleeping in the snow's embrace.

Ah! the Furs in which your nakedness retires,
Exacerbating my inflamed desires!
And from the bruisèd bareness of your flesh
Rise hot betrayals and unknown caprice,
And my winter soul, lost in its solemn quest,
Sinks in the faithless fragrance of the golden Fleece.

Departure

La lampe des longs soirs projette un rayon d'ambre

The twilit lamplight casts an amber glow
Which blurs the gilding of the picture frames.
The hour for my going has sounded in the chamber ...
The night is dark, I can't see past the panes.

I no longer know the faces of the things
That witnessed good and bad not long ago ...
See, the roses' familiar scent is dying ...
The night is dark, I know not where I go.

Should I regret that other time? ... Perhaps ...
Yet I need no regrets nor feel their lack ...
I walk before myself, the future is my master,
And, whatever be my fate, I shall not come back.

Pillory

Pendant longtemps, je fus clouée au pilori

For a long time, I was chained to the pillory.
Women saw my suffering and laughed at me.

Then, men hurled clods of mire from the street,
Which spattered on my temples and my cheek.

Tears rose up, a throbbing undertow,
but I choked back the sobbing in my throat.

I saw them there, as though a fearful dream
Whose terrors lengthen and whose horrors teem.

The place was public, all were come to see.
The women flung their giggling at me.

They threw their rotten fruits, they chanted sneering songs,
The wind bore vicious whispers toward me in my bonds.

Their rage invaded, and their fear appalled.
In silence there, I learned to hate them all.

Their insults stung, as though a nettle's lash.
When they unchained me, I was free at last.

I was free to follow where the north winds led ...
Since then, I've borne the visage of the dead.

LITANY OF HATE

La Haine nous unit, plus forte que l'Amour.

The tie that binds us, more than Love, is Hate.
We hate the smirking song-and-dance of day,
The sunlit springtime's harsh returning gaze.

We hate the aggressivity of the male.
We share the last regrets, the bitter gasps for air
Of Women empty-eyed and Women pale.

We hate the brutish rut that soils desire.
We shun it as anathema, the cry
In which the unborn sorrows of life are sired.

We hate the Law, the World, the thronging Crowd.
A feral voice come growling into town,
Our revolution shudders and resounds.

Lover-less lovers, husbandless wives,
Lilith has breathed her shadow in our lives,
And on our lips the kiss of Eblis lies.

My mistress, lovelier than Love, is Hate.
I covet her cruel priestess in your shape
Whose ecstasy my rage exacerbates.

Twining greenwood's gold with iris dark as night,
We shall renounce the tears of the contrite,
The penitence of lilies and of candlelight.

I'll leave those sleepy homes unvisited.
Scents are rising toward me, dark and dread,
And memories of the martyred Women dead.

THE GRAZERS OF GRASS

C'est l'heure où l'âme famélique des repus

Now is the hour when the souls of beasts
Starve to death among their rotten feasts.

The Grazers of Grass have honed the teeth they wield
On flowers blooming in October fields,

The wood-brown fields, where hobnails rust to stubs …
They drink the dewdrops up with long glub-glubs.

The darkened summer, jealous, has withdrawn,
And the Grazers of Grass have deflowered the lawn.

They chew the honey-clover, and, for seconds,
The fields of chickory more blue than Heaven.

Innocent, just like the little lambs of Holy Writ,
They ruminate in burblings of spit.

Indifferent to the buzzing of the flies,
They never raise their greedy glutton-eyes.

And, more overbearing than a host of victory calls,
The greasy noise of chewing rises from their jaws.

Above the Public Place

Les nuages flottants déroulaient leur écharpe

The drifting clouds unfurled in the pure sky
As though a scarf the soft gray-blue of linen.
I was young and fervent, and I had a harp.
The world appeared to me, soft and feminine.

In the woods, gray amaranthine violets
Made my wide eyes rejoice. The laugh
Of Irish shepherds' wandering hearts and souls
Welled up within me, from the distant past.

The tree-sap filled me with many a drunkenness,
And I drank up that marvelous wine, uncaring.
I wandered with my harp and its great promise
And knew not what a treasure I was bearing.

One day, I followed the women and the men
Toward the blue-roofed city. I went down,
From dark and fiery woods, to follow them,
And I bore my harp all through the town.

And then I sang above the public place
From which a stench of rotten fish was stirring,
But, intoxicated with my music's sound,
I did not hear the market's murmuring.

For I remembered all that the wise trees
Had told me, in the silence of the woods.
All around, the catcalls and the whistles
Mingled with the hawking of their goods.

A woman saw me, offered me her hand
In the mob shrieking out its greed and wrath,
But, borne away by the summons of a breeze,
She disappeared at the turning of the path.

I sang sincerely: so all shepherds sing.
All around, the vile noise was waning,
And, as the sunset cast its firelight,
I saw I was alone and day was fading.

I sang without a witness, for the joy
Of singing, as one does when love takes flight,
When hope mocks, when oblivion destroys.
The harp broke under my hands, in the night.

I'll Say This …

O si le Seigneur penchait son front sur mon trépas

If, when I am dead, the Lord should come to see,
I'd tell him, "Christ, you didn't die for me.

"O Lord, your rigid law was never mine.
I lived as though a pagan in an ancient time.

"You see the innocence in which I lived.
I do not know you, and I never did.

"I flowed like water, I fled like the sand.
If I sinned, never did I understand.

"Around me was the world in its first blush.
I drank the crystal light of dawn and dusk.

"The brightest sunbeams circled me, and yes,
Love bade me look for women's loveliness.

"You see, the sky spread wide, awakening.
A virgin came to me. And I was waiting.

"Night fell … Then morning took us by surprise,
Sullenly, with its dull, sullen light.

"And in my clasping arms, she slept as when
Women sleep, clasped in the arms of their men.

"Since then, I've lived maddened and unmanned,
Seeking eternity in single grains of sand.

"I didn't see how cold, how cruel she was,
And I loved that woman, in spite of your laws.

"Since I sought only love, I was despised
By men of worth — and all for her bright eyes.

"No longer did I listen to the voice I loved,
For I had learned that no one would be moved.

"However, night is falling, and my mortal name
Is fading, for the world will have its claim.

"Dreams of bright tomorrows, too, have come to dust:
No one will whisper my verses, toward dusk.

"Now, Lord, judge me. For we stand
Here, face to face, in the silence of man.

"If my love was sweet, it was bitter as well,
And I have deserved neither heaven nor hell.

"I didn't learn the hymns of the angelic throng,
For, long ago, I'd heard those other songs,

"The songs of Lesbos, which are silent now.
Before your virtues, I remain unbowed.

"But I never attempted rebellion: a kiss
Was all the blasphemy upon my lips.

"Then let me hasten toward the twilight blue
And join the women who have never known you!

"Sappho, fingers wandering over her silent lyre,
Will marvel at the virgin I desire,

"And the one I love will seem to her
More lily-pale than Atthis and more pure.

"And we, the silent chorus, shall not stir,
We'll hear the voice that Mytilene heard,

"While flowers brighten in the torches' flame ...
For, in a bitter world, we dared to speak her name.

"Lying on the gold and silken couch,
She poured out nectar to rejoice the mouth.

"And she will sing, in language bright and free,
The Lesbian bower opening on the sea,

"The bower humming with cicadas, where
The scent of grapevines vibrates in the air.

"Our gowns will ripple among the white peplos
Of Atthis and Timas, and Eranna of Telos,

"Those whose radiant names alone enthrall,
Around the singing Aede, one and all!

"You see, already close to those last, fatal throes,
I dare to speak to you, whom no one knows.

"Forgive me — your religion wasn't mine!
Let me go toward that splendid, ancient time

"And (since at last Eternity is coming true)
Rejoin those women whom you never knew."

THE LATENT NIGHT

Le soir, doux berger, développe

The dusk, a gentle shepherd, sings
Its rustic solo tune ...
I chew a sprig of heliotrope
Like Fra Diavolo, and soon
The smoke-fumes of the latent night
Spark, a dark Vesuvius alight,
With kiln-smoke veiling all the white
Bright aureole of the moon.

I am the fervent follower
Of the dusk and of the sea.
Lust, unique and multiple,
In my mirror looks at me ...
I'm sorry for my clown-like face.
I seek your corpse, your resting-place,
A haven, calm and full of grace,
O my lovely Misery!

Ah! the cold of hand in hand
Beneath the marble, here with you,
Beneath the heavy earth anointed
With the tree-sap and the dew!
My soul, which agony exalts,
Approaches, languishing, to halt
Before these columns of basalt
With all their viaduct-blue.

When analysis explores
The gaping chasm of the night,
In my revolt convulses, spasms,
A giant's fury and his might.
And, weary of fair, false renown,
Of joy in which the spirit drowns,
I turn away and I bow down
Before your void so glossy-bright.

SHE PASSES

Le ciel l'encadre ainsi que ferait une châsse

The sky encases her like relic-ashes,
And centuries could go by without a sight
Of her. She is the miracle of night.
The holy moment glows and chimes. She passes …

I have come here with the leprous throng,
Before the dawn, and knowing I'll be healed.
They gaze on her, as on the truth revealed,
Weeping low. I weep along with them.

In the air, a ray of bright hope flashes,
For her bare feet have sanctified the path.
A lily-flower's fallen from her hand …
The sobs go still. She passes.

She's made her saints of all who wept, abashed,
And now among us no one is afraid.
She will not come again along this way,
But I no longer suffer, since I saw her pass.

Song

Ta chevelure d'un blond rose

Like a golden rose, your hair
Is splendid as the setting sun,
Your silence seems a loveable
Pause within a lovely song.

And you pass by, O my Belovèd,
In breezes shivering and fresh ...
My spirit bears the heaven-scent
Of the white roses of your flesh.

When you raise your lashes, then
Your pale eyes, a subtle blue,
Reflect the flowers' long, low light,
And — *April!* — they are calling you.

WAIT

En cette chambre où meurt un souvenir d'aveux

A memory is dying here, and in the air
Yesterday's jasmine scent has gone astray ...
For you I have put on this fine array,
For you alone have I unbound my hair.

I have chosen jewels ... will they delight?
My heart goes still, my heart beats anxiously ...
How shall I seem to you, what will you say to me,
My love, when you unclose my door tonight?

Ocean violets shall pour down before us
Within the green and violet windowpane ...
And, in suspense, I taste the perfect pain:
The wait for joys that only come at dusk.

In silence, I await the hour I envision ...
Night passes, trailing light and shadows, by ...
My boundless soul is scattered in the sky ...
The air is mild, and see: the moon has risen.

WORDS TO MY LOVE

Tu me comprends: je suis un être médiocre

You understand me: I am mediocre,
Not good, not very bad, calm, a little sly.
I hate strong perfumes and the voice raised high,
And gray is more to me than red or ochre.

I love the dying day extinguished gradually,
The fire, the cloistered closeness of a chamber
Where lampshades, veiling their transparent amber,
Blush red the bronze and blue the pottery.

My eyes upon the rug more worn than sand,
I lazily evoke the gold-grained shore,
The glimmers of the drifting tides of yore ...
And nonetheless, I bear a guilty brand.

You see: I'm at the age the virgin yields her hand
To the man her weakness seeks and fears,
And I have no companion for my years,
Since you appeared just at the pathway's bend.

The hyacinth was bleeding on the scarlet glen,
You dreamt, while Love went walking by your side ...
Women have no right to beauty. I'd
Been banished to the ugliness of men.

And I had the terrible audacity to yearn
For sister-love, of bright, white, pure light,
The gentle voice uniting with the night,
The furtive step that doesn't break the fern.

Your eyes, your hair had been forbidden me,
Because your hair is long and full of fragrant scents,
Because your eyes have fires so intense
They cloud themselves, like the rebellious sea.

They pointed fingers in their rage at me,
Because my eyes looked for your gentle eyes …
No one, to see us pass, would recognize
That I had chosen you in all simplicity.

Think on the vile law that I transgress,
And judge my love, which knows no evil will,
As honest, as essential, and as fatal still
As any man's desire for his mistress.

They did not read the brightness in my gaze
Upon the path whereto my fortune led …
"Who is that damned woman" (so they said)
"Toward whom the flames of Hell so deafly blaze?"

Let's leave them to their impure moralities,
For dawn is gold as honey and as bright,
And unembittered days, and better nights
Will come, the friends who put our minds at ease …

Let's watch the brightness of the stars above …
What matters it, to us, man's judgment from afar?
And what have we to fear, knowing that we are
Pure in this life and knowing that we love … ?

Toward Lesbos

Tu viendras, les yeux pleins du soir et de l'hier ...

The twilight in your eyes, you'll come to me
Just as the sun goes down beyond the sea.

Frail as a cradle bobbing on the tide,
Our ship will carry spices and amber inside.

Our sails will billow with the west wind's gust.
"Tonight," I'll say, "the sea belongs to us."

Like petals, your fingers will be long and pale.
We'll travel at random, the wind in our sails.

Raising frightened eyes, you'll ask in alarm,
"In what unknown bed shall I sleep in your arms?"

Concealed among the sails, some birds will sing.
The stars will rise, the darkness will set in.

"Beneath my fingers' touch, the ripples bend ...
Along what strange strand will our pilgrimage end?"

But — "The sea grows pale at night," I'll softly say,
"And the island I love is still far, far away.

"Now close your weary eyes, and sleep as deep
As in your own closed room, and I the watch shall keep.

"Like a woman who sings in a bower at dusk,
On that island, there's happiness waiting for us.

"Veil your pale face with your long, auburn hair.
The heavens are cloudless, and calm is the air.

"Above all, do not fear ... for we're safe from the flood,
From the risks of the winds and the waters, my Love ..."

The silver crescent as your talisman,
You'll sleep until the rising of the sun.

The shores will trace a margin, imperceptibly,
Against the clouds ... Your eyes will open on the sea.

You'll question me, and not without some fear.
Mysterious songs will murmur in your ears ...

You'll whisper, blushing like a little girl,
"Those unknown voices have a strange allure.

"Their sigh soothes my weariness like a woman's fan:
But the dawn is still dark, and I don't understand.

"Our unhappy fate — will it lie far below
This sad, fearful day I see starting to glow?

And I will say, closing your lips with a kiss,
"Our joy lies below ... We must dare even this ...

"Below, we'll listen to the last, best theme ...
And, see, we're approaching the island of dreams ..."

SAPPHO LIVES AGAIN

La lune se levait autrefois à Lesbos

The moon rose over Lesbos in the dark
Above the waking women-lovers.
Love, rising slowly from the sleeping waters,
Went sobbing in the lyre's deepest heart.

Sappho bound her brow with violets
To honor Eros, who came streaming down
Among the oaks ... and Atthis's violet crown
Shone brighter yet amid the torches' light.

The shores were blazing, blond with golden sand ...
The virgins taught the pretty foreign girls
The lithe and light caresses Night prefers,
And sea and sky spread out along the strand.

... Some few among us have preserved the rites
That once set Lesbos glowing like an altar-flame.
We know Love is a pleasurable pain,
Our lovers have the Graces' small white feet.

Our bodies mirror theirs. The night grows still.
Our sisters, pure as snow in spring: they know,
They know the strange, soft way, so long ago,
That Sappho could bend Atthis to her will.

With infinite simplicity, we adore them
In all the wonderment of wide-eyed children
To whom the world's eternal gold is given ...
In our music, Sappho lives again.

Our kisses move as soft as willowbuds,
And our embraces hold a cold, pale fire;
We touch our lovers as we would a lyre ...
Our love is greater than all other loves.

And we repeat the words of Sappho, when
Our hearts, beneath the silver moon, go ranging:
"O lovely girls, toward you I am unchanging."
The ones we love have scorned the race of men.

Our moonlit kisses nor our fingers' touch
Could ever bruise their lips or scratch their cheeks,
And, when their gowns have fallen, we can be
Their lovers and their sisters, both at once.

Lust, in us, is less than warmth and light.
And yet a child's love was our undoing,
Since Aphrodite willed it so, approving
That all of us remain her acolytes.

In our bodies, Sappho lives again;
Like her, we've heard the sirens' song,
And, like hers, our souls are calm and strong,
We who never heed the scorn of passing men.

Fervently, we pray: "Prolong the night
For us, whose kisses fear the dawn, for us
Whose thighs are open in our mortal lust,
Who are one flesh and blinded by its light ..."

Our mistresses could never do us wrong,
For, in their forms, we love infinity ...
And since their kisses grant us immortality,
We have no fear of Hell's oblivion.

And so we sing, and our souls overflow.
Our days, with neither sorrow nor remorse,
Uncurl themselves like long, melodious chords,
And we love, as they loved on Lesbos long ago.

THE SILENT FLUTE

Je m'écoute, avec des frissons ardents

Ardently I listen to my singing,
The little faun with timid eyes and proud.
The soul of woodlands dwells between my teeth,
The god of rhythm lives within my mouth.

In this forest, far from prowling Pan,
My heart is sweeter than a rose in bloom;
The rays of sunlight, charged with happy scents,
Dance to the music of the verdant flute.

Mingle your tresses, join fair arm in arm,
While at your feet, the ram snorts in the hay,
Ye hedgeland nymphs! Oh, come not near!
Go take your laughter elsewhere while I play!

I hold my sacred art reserved, apart.
In honor of the haughty Muse I follow,
I will seek the shade, and I will hide
My thrilling pipes within an oak tree's hollow.

And I will play, in shadows and in scents,
The livelong day, while waiting for the time
Of rowdy choruses and common games
And naked breasts the night breeze brushes by ...

And yet my loyal, holy song I still
While the festival exults in firelight.
Only the night wind will know my pain,
The trees alone will witness my delight.

So I guard my lovely times from you
Whose goat-eyes spy upon my lonely trysts,
My friends! Go laugh somewhere else
While this singing flowers on my lips!

If not, well then, I'm a faun, after all,
And as for any billy-goat who bucks,
Then I'll avenge myself with hooves and horns,
With one good blow I'll lay him in the dust!

ROSES RISEN

Ma brune aux yeux dorés, ton corps d'ivoire et d'ambre

Dark woman, golden-eyed, of ivory and amber,
Your luminescent shimmer makes the chamber
Beyond the garden shine.

The midnight sky, behind my eyelids closed,
Still glows ... and I drink in the perfume of the rose
More red than wine.

Abandoning their vines, the roses rise.
I drink their short-lived sigh, I breathe their lives.
All wholly, they abound.

By miracle ... the stars have entered in,
Hasting through the shattered windowpane
Whose molten gold poured down.

Now, among the roses and the stars,
Unveiled, within my chamber, here you are,
Your nakedness alight.

And in my eyes alights your gaze's wordless gleam ...
With neither stars nor flowers now, I dream
In the cold, cold night.

ENTER MY REALM

Entre dans mon royaume, envahis mon empire.

Enter my realm, make my kingdom your thrall.
There are columns of porphyry in the great hall ...
There we shall celebrate luminous feasts,
And we shall rejoice with the lordly deceased
And their ladies, dead and entrancing.

Princesses, queens, and women-lovers, dancing,
Parading and laughing, as in their glory days,
Shall clothe themselves, for us, in their glorious arrays.
Look, see them there, magnificent, serene,
The women who were Queens.

The procession of prophets and kings begins to flow,
Wearing their purple robes of long ago.
Do you not know them, those moonlit spirits there,
Dark Anne Boleyn, Rosamund the fair,
And Bess with auburn hair?

See, before your sweet and haughty stare,
Singing, weeping, laughing, those who reigned above,
All who were lovely, all who were loved.
The fountains, in among their jets, flame bright,
Your people to delight.

A priest shall crown you with a golden band.
Before that great assemblage, hear me: I command
That all here, from now on, submit to you,
That your vows be my vows, my friends your allies too,
O royal will!

Enter this cathedral, cross the threshold's sill,
This edifice raised from my dreams at night.
The nave has been adorned to welcome you aright.
Enter, beneath the dome-like vaulting, you who reign,
Queen of my domain.

Teaching

Tu veux savoir de moi le secret des sorcières?

You would learn the witches' secret rite?
Then I will light their lanterns just for you tonight,
And I will tell you of the witches' simple rite.

The witches sleep by day and live by night.
Their eyes flee from the daybreak's blinding light,
Accustomed to the shadows of the night.

The witches' souls are very calm and dark,
The starlight is less strange to them than Carnival.
The planets' flame lights up their pupils' dark.

We fear them, and we hunt them: we do not find them good.
They fled the common meal and the neighborhood.
They did not understand, they are not understood.

But they are very simple ... One is born a witch ...
To understand them, you must get to know them a bit,
And know their right to be, and to be born a witch ...

We speak so loftily of good and wickedness.
We know how gravely wrong their deviancy is ...
And yet their hearts could not conceive of wickedness.

But those women are damned, and foreign as well.
For it's a heavy world in which their light souls dwell,
And their laws will forever be foreign, as well.

They barely touch the soil — and so light!
The things they love are either black or white,
Or else the shade that shimmers in the light.

In their gaze, and in their smiles' ambiguity,
Dull gold and darkened purple, the rags of royalty,
Array their forms in splendid ambiguity.

And they know how to hide, from the hard glare of Day,
Their hearts, their tragic love, and their despondent hate,
And their spirits untouched by the beauty of Day.

What does it matter if, when they are overcome,
By the powers of Day, the songs they lived among
Be silenced like the last cry of the overcome ... ?

What does it matter? — They are all uncaring.
This world is but an instrument they're playing,
Which sobs beneath their hands, sweet and uncaring.

Like the Moon, they live in dreams, alone,
Choosing, on this Earth, to call their own
The lands where lonely souls can die alone.

For One

Quelqu'un, je crois, se souviendra
dans l'avenir de nous.
Mon Souci.
— Sappho

Someone, I think, will remember us
in the days to come.
My Care.
— Sappho

In the future gray as an uncertain dawn,
Someone, I think, will remember us,
While autumn burns above the amber fields
With eyes of rust.

Just one among the beings on this earth,
O my Desire! will remember us,
A woman, whose brow will bear the mystery
Of love and lust.

She will love the rippling in the olive trees,
The seaspray in its light and leaping arc,
The flowers of the snow and of the sea,
The winter and the dark.

And, bidding shores and riversides farewell,
Beneath the sunlight's somber, solemn glare,
She will know the sacred love of virgins,
Atthis, my Care.

EPITAPH

Voici la porte d'où je sors ...

This is the door I leave you by ...
O my roses and my thorns!
Before — what does it signify?
I sleep, and dream of holy things ...

Here, then, ravished in delight,
My soul lies, safe and sound, at rest,
Having, for the love of Death,
Absolved the crime — of Life.

Acknowledgments

I first encountered Renée Vivien in anthologies edited by Norman Shapiro, Terry Castle, and Lillian Faderman, and, soon afterward, in the "Lesbian Immortal" seminar taught by Professor Kate Thomas of Bryn Mawr College. The faculty of the English and French Departments at Bryn Mawr and the Comparative Literature Program at the University of Pennsylvania have supported me in this and other interests. I owe a particular debt of gratitude to Professor Mario Maurin, who offered line-by-line critiques of my first efforts at translating French poetry into English. To his spouse, Professor Grace Armstrong: please know that Professor Maurin's kindness and generosity will not be forgotten. With the encouragement of my mentors, I sent a query email to the poet Cristie Cyane, who graciously put me in touch with Imogen Bright, Renée Vivien's great-niece. Ms. Bright has generously provided a wealth of information on Vivien's life and work, and it was she who suggested that I read Jean-Paul Goujon's biography and Virginie Sanders's literary analysis. Thank you all, from my heart.

My thanks to the editors of the following publications in which these Vivien translations first appeared, or will appear soon:

Adrienne: "Victory," "Desire," "Prophecy," "Roses Risen"
Gertrude: "The Drowned Women" and "Furs"
Lavender Review: "The Silent Flute"
PMS (poemmemoirstory): "Above the Public Place"

About the Translator

Samantha Pious received her A.B. in English at Bryn Mawr College and is currently pursuing a Ph.D. in Comparative Literature at the University of Pennsylvania. Her specialties are medieval courtly poetry and women's writing. She sees herself more as a product of the fin-de-siècle than the turn of this millennium, and she is drawn to Renée Vivien out of a shared sense of anachronism, in terms of poetic style as well as subject matter. *A Crown of Violets,* a finalist for the Charlotte Mew Prize, is her first book.

About the Author

Renée Vivien (née Pauline Mary Tarn, 1877-1909) was an English expatriate who made her home in Paris during the Belle Époque. In 1903, Vivien's collection of translations and adaptations from the Ancient Greek poetry of Sappho became one of the first works of modern European lesbian literature to be published by a lesbian writer under her real name. This courageous act was the death-sentence of her literary career. Parisian critics who had praised the mysterious "R. Vivien" as a young man of poetic genius began to snub at first and then simply ignore the newly un-closeted woman poet. Even in the face of ridicule and disrespect, Vivien continued to write and publish poetry, short stories, translations, plays, epigrams, and a novel based on her real-life romances with Natalie Clifford Barney and the Baroness Hélène van Zuylen van Nyevelt van Haar (née Rothschild).

Further Reading

The original French texts of the translations in this collection may be found in *Lavender Review* 12 (December 2015) at the following URL: « http://www.lavrev.net/2015/12/renee-vivien.html ». We have included first-line epigraphs in the print volume for ease of reference.

French Editions

Vivien, Renée. *Poèmes 1901-1910.* ed. Nicole G. Albert. ErosOnyx, 2009.

— — —. *Poésies complètes.* ed. Jean-Paul Goujon. Régine Deforges, 1986.

— — —. *Les Kitharèdes.* ed. Marie-Jo Bonnet. ErosOnyx, 2008.

— — —. *Sapho.* ErosOnyx, 2009.

Anthologies and Translations

Castle, Terry, ed. *The Literature of Lesbianism: A Historical Anthology From Ariosto to Stonewall.* New York: Columbia University Press, 2005. 608-613.

Caws, Mary Ann, ed. & trans. *The Yale Anthology of Twentieth-Century French Poetry.* New Haven: Yale University Press, 2004. 107-108.

Faderman, Lillian, ed. *Chloe Plus Olivia: An Anthology of Lesbian Literature from the Seventeenth Century to the Present.* 2nd edition. New York: Penguin Books, 1995.

Schultz, Gretchen, and Anne Atik, eds. *An Anthology of Nineteenth-Century Women's Poetry from France; in English Translation, with French Text.* New York: Modern Language Association of America, 2008.

Shapiro, Norman, ed. & trans. *French Women Poets of Nine Centuries: The   Distaff and the Pen.* Baltimore: Johns Hopkins University Press,   2008. 868-875.

Spraggs, Gillian, ed. & trans. *Love Shook My Senses: Lesbian Love Poems.* London: The Women's Press, 1998.

Vivien, Renée. *A Woman Appeared to Me.* Trans. Jeannette H. Foster. ed. Gayle Rubin. Bates City: Naiad Press, 1976.

— — —. *At The Sweet Hour of Hand in Hand.* Trans. Sandia Belgrade. Ed. Bonnie Poucel. Bates City: Naiad Press, 1979.

— — —. *The Muse of the Violets: Poems.* Trans. Margaret Porter and Catherine Kroger. Bates City: Naiad Press, 1977.

— — —. *The Woman of the Wolf and Other Stories.* Trans. Karla Jay and Yvonne M. Klein. New York: Gay Presses, 1983.

Biography and Criticism

Albert, Nicole G., ed. *Renée Vivien à rebours: Études pour un centenaire.* Paris: Orizons, 2009.

— — —. *Renée Vivien: Une femme de lettres entre deux siècles (1877-1909).* Paris: Honoré Champion, 2012.

Benstock, Shari. *Women of the Left Bank: Paris, 1900-1940.* Austin: University of Texas Press, 1986.

Goujon, Jean-Paul. *Tes blessures sont plus douces que leurs caresses: Vie de Renée Vivien.* Régine Deforges, 1986.

Sanders, Virginie. *La poésie de Renée Vivien: "Vertigineusement, j'allais vers les Étoiles ... "* Amsterdam: RoJopi, 1991.

Headmistress Press Books

On Loving a Saudi Girl
Carina Yun

The Burn Poems
Lynn Strongin

I Carry My Mother
Lesléa Newman

Distant Music
Joan Annsfire

The Awful Suicidal Swans
Flower Conroy

Joy Street
Laura Foley

Chiaroscuro Kisses
G.L. Morrison

The Lillian Trilogy
Mary Meriam

Lady of the Moon
Amy Lowell
Lillian Faderman
Mary Meriam

Irresistible Sonnets
Lavender Review
ed. Mary Meriam

Printed in Great Britain
by Amazon